FOR EVERY ROAD

The Journey of a Hedge Bard

**Poetry and Lyrics by
Ted MacGillivray**

Publication per Scriptor
1765 Oyster Way
Gabriola Island,
British Columbia V0R 1X6

Library and Archives Canada Cataloguing in Publication

MacGillivray, Ted, author
For Every Road: it's all about choices / Ted MacGillivray;
Includes index. Poems and lyrics.

ISBN 978-0-9939478-0-3 (pbk.)

I. Title. PS8625.G5454F67 2015 C813'.6 C2015-901841-2

Edited by Bernice Lever
Typeset by Mary Jane Jessen
Fonts: Arno Pro, Frutiger Next Pro

Dedicated
with much love
to Alice, Sage and Heather

Some Previous Publications

Suite Sixteen (songs, including lead sheets)
Winterland (a song cycle including lead sheets)
The Motion Picture in Business (AMPPL)

Selections published in
The Oestara Anthology of Pagan Poetry
Sing and String
The Web

Films
(writer, director, producer)
16th Floor (soft drugs and family) (Uniroyal)
Thrill Drivers (Dunlop)
This is Horseracing (CBC)
Death of a Christian (funeral customs) and
The Royal Door (Orthodox Christianity) for CBC
"Heritage" (religious) series.
Electronics in Canada
Kananaskis Country Holiday (Alberta Parks)
William Watson Lodge (Alberta Parks)
River Reborn (Albert Parks)
Stormy Angel (Uniroyal)
Coffee House Test

Contents

Foreword

THIS BOOK exists because my wife, Alice Elizabeth MacGillivray PhD, née Windebank, Bill (Wm. Lloyd) Hay MD, and others insisted. My love of language came from my father, a gentleman and a decorated WWI officer who wrote stunning letters to his sister, my aunt, Elizabeth M. Marlowe, describing his wartime experiences. She transcribed his longhand so I could read them. Dad died when I was 10 years old (my mother had died when I was two) and my aunt sent me to boarding schools, her motives as much about reestablishing our family as they were about giving me intellectual tools.

My extended family did everything possible to discourage me from following the arts, which, during the '30s depression, made some sense. But, through my musically-talented mother, my maternal grandfather, Peter Rutherford, an artist and musician, bequeathed me his talents, and his wife, Annie Orchard Rutherford, a suffragette and a founder of the United Church, the Women's College Hospital, Canada's first women's hospital, and the Women's Christian Temperance Union, left me a social conscience and a model of determination. Studying theatre at Hart House (UofT) I learned that artists were a caste removed from general society. And as I have found since, the more one lives as an artist, the farther one gets from the mainstream.

Vive La Compagnie

Hail to our companions on the Road
wiry carnivores who dream the world a kinder place
yet lick their scarlet wounds in sweet surprise
at the rich, gold-speckled warmth
of their own ancestral, ocean-salty blood.

— Ted.

I'VE HAD SO MANY FRIENDS, supporters, patrons, partners, associates, critics and teachers, that I'm at a loss to name them all. Sadly, some of them are only memories, but others, I thank the Gods, are still here. My heartfelt gratitude to:

Alice MacGillivray, Sage MacGillivray, Earl Barlow, Sterndale Bennett, Christine MacLeod Binkley, Tony Braden, Len Chandler, Jeannie Chappel, Janet Churnin, Sid Dolgay, Bob Gill, Ronwen Guest, Marion Harris (my singing partner), Bill Hay MD, Casey (Crawford) Jones MD, Charles Jordan, Brian Jupe, Gerry Keeley, Bernice Lever, Dick Lewis, Blake (my Dad) MacGillivray, Elizabeth M. Marlowe (my aunt), Ed Mitchell (Camp of the Blue Ox), Susan Musgrave, Linda Rogers, Ed Rollins, Trix Schilte, Ruth Stirling, Bill Thorsteinson, Naomi Wakan, Zalman Yanovsky.

And the great explorers who have inspired me, such as Bucky Fuller, who acknowledged me as a comprehensivist, John Cunningham Lilly (whom I've never met but who led me in the exploration of my own mind), Marshall McLuhan, the master of media and synthesis, and the writings of Aleister Crowley.

U2

(a sensitive new-age guy's love poem)

I would chase you up a ladder to the heavens
(with your consent of course)
yet never grabbing your ankle
until on the roof of the world
you turned to face me.

I would chase you down the caverns of abysmus
(with your consent of course)
yet never touching your shoulder
until at the core of the universe
you turned to embrace me.

I would chase you through the star-trails of the cosmos
(with your consent of course)
rocking and rolling and diving and soaring
back to back and belly to belly
yet never touching your body
until, at the source of everything
you turned to enspace me.

SeaThing

And the thunder surf is heedless of the sand it sweeps before it
As it crashes on the beaches and it booms against the jetties.
And the tide hands sweep in triumph to the thresholds of the cities
And it lingers in the tide pools and trickles back reluctant
And it feels no fear or anger as it ebbs away by moonlight
And the ocean can't remember all the times that she has been there.

And the tide comes in at noonday as gentle as a swallow
And it laps against the pilings and caresses ships at anchor
And it lurks outside the harbour, mother home to life eternal
Waiting for the moment when the moon drives her to madness
And rage will overtake her as she screams in naked laughter
And the ocean can't remember all the times that she has been there.

And her moods are gray and angry or cool and deep and distant
As she crushes tiny freighters and casts up vacant bodies.
And she never offers mercy and she never offers quarter
And she never asks forgiveness and she never tells her story
And she swallows men regardless of their timeless tries to tame her
And the ocean can't remember all the times that she has been there.

And time is working for her as the white clouds fall as raindrops
And she drinks the mountain waters from the lips of endless rivers
And the seabirds must land sometime
                                        on the foam breast's warm horizon
And the fishes eat the seaweed as they themselves are eaten
And the waves wash on forever on a thousand other planets
And the ocean can't remember all the times that she has been there.

And the starfish stud the sandbars where the pirate gold lies buried
With the soldier's rusted rifle and a blacksmith's broken hammer
And the priest's encrusted censer and the martyr's cross of sainthood
And the pharaoh's weathered tombstone and the virgin's belt of iron
And the baby's rotted nipple and the poet's musty verses
And the ocean can't remember all the times that she has been there.

Shaitan's Priest

Tell me, Reverend Father,
why did you change your gown?
So worn and torn the old one
it made me seem a clown.

Tell me, Reverend Father
why did you change your name?
I needed something similar
that wasn't quite the same.

Tell me Reverend Father
of the churches you have built.
I die each time I take their coin,
take on myself their guilt.

Tell me, Reverend Father
why do you take their gold?
To live today I'd rather,
eternal life I've sold.

Tell me, Reverend Father,
when did you lose your soul?
The day I learned that living
was life's eternal goal.

Tell me Reverend Father,
when did you change your church?
The day I saw an altar
implicit in a couch.

Remembrance

Strolling through the shattered autumn leaves,
oak and maple, yellow, red and brown,
the prince consults his golden timepiece (wound
sometime each day by silent, unseen slaves),
and sees himself his grandsire picking through
decaying corpses on a battlefield,
his steel-shod, armored horse disquiet at
the beauty and bouquet of rotting flesh.
His the day and his the field and yet
he wonders idly why he has no thought
or feeling for that refuse on the ground
who fought and died to win for him the game.
But after all he'd owned them; they were his
to use and spend or squander as he chose.

Don't Look at the Elephants

Don't look at the elephants. Just ignore them.
Turn your head away. Pretend you can't smell them
or feel the weight of their body heat.
And there's no oppression; you can move with
absolute freedom if you just avoid their feet
by peeking carefully before you step.
Oh, and don't lift your arms too high because
you might touch their wrinkled skin
and that sparse, coarse hair.
And if you keep your breathing really shallow
you won't take more than your share of the oxygen.
That wouldn't be fair, and besides, someone might notice.
And don't ever, ever mention them, even in a joke,
because they'll come and lock you away in a pastel room
with no one to talk to and nothing to read
and give you pills and electricity
till the elephants and everything just become
shadows on the wall.

Vista I

High on the Misty Mountain
where forest firs
brood in shadowy silence
time slows.

Deep in the sunny valley
where village homes
hum in summer comfort
time flows.

Far in the smoky city
where neon towers
crowd in stony clamour
time flies.

High on the misty mountain
where feather clouds
cling in whispering shyness
time dies.

Vista II

Beyond the misty mountain
stand the silent peaks
where snow never melts,
where veiled clouds hang
and the crisp dry wind
whips and curls around
crags and promontories
where no one stands.

It is cold on the silent peaks.
In their towering chill
no life stirs
but the timeless and crystalline musings
Of the Goddess' mind.

Vista III

Beyond the Misty Mountain
and the snow-capped peaks,
metaphysical energy glows
crystalline, shimmering
left-right, back-forth
in-out, on-off,
binary, its sum 0,
zero,
nothing,
everything,
silver somehow
against the scattered blue sky.

Why such awesome beauty
in the seething, struggling
mass of life
feeding on itself
each other --
such ugliness, such beauty,
such ecstasy, such horror,
and we part of it?

Who Needs You

(from a suggestion by the late Bill McMurtry QC)

Who needs you? Who wants you?
Who'll feed you? Who'll clothe you?
Are you good enough to make it,
Are you strong enough to take it,
Are you smart enough to fake it,
Whatcha gonna do
in a world where food grows scarcer
and great machines can do the work
that used to be the life and lot of men,
ask yourself this question if you dare
Who needs you? Who wants you?
Anywhere?

Who owns the land?
Who owns the earth on which you stand?
Who charges rent
for space to rest your head or pitch your tent?
Who claims a piece of holy earth to say
that anyone who walks on it must pay?

Who owns the tools?
Who writes the laws and makes the rules?
Who gives you bread
because your worth is greater (a)live than dead?
Who sells the food for which you slave?
Who owns your days from womb to grave?

Who owns the guns?
Who buys the weakest of our sons?
Who pays the bills
for dogs so insecure they'll hire to kill?
Who will shoe your pretty little feet,
Who will glove your hand?
Who will rape your mind and body,
Take your change to pay the piper
And the Big Brass Band?

Who needs you?

Courtship

A red rose, lonely, living past its time,
stardust sprinkled from an autumn sky.
A wolf, returned to peaceful domesticity,
my soul-era father lays to rest his pistol
beside my nurse musician mother's camera,
speaks in words of love and hopeful splendor
while she, receptive as her camera's lens,
listens and encourages.

Untitled

All my life I've hoped to meet
a woman I could love in flesh and mind
but all in vain

For men are such deluded creatures --
see the way our bodies rule our brains
and make us blind.

Times I've danced to love's illusion,
kissed a breast so fair, a rose so fine.
Times I've chanced the awful fusion,
shared a mind the Goddess had designed.
My, how time flies.

So I search your whirlpool eyes
looking for the spark that brands the wise.

Light Waves

Light waves
an endless
patterns repeating
shine in the glowing
cathedral darkness
transparent to stars
a space in space.

Light waves
of white caps
of stars rushing
through mouths of the cavern
a feather-soft surf
evaporates lightly
flows back so quietly
leaving inviolate
this place in place.

Light shafts
rebound
echo like sound
reflections from matter
substance insubstantial
shimmer in craglets
intergrace facelets
formed by the flashing
of light upon nothing
darkness beyond
in darkness resounding
face interface.

Shadows

Shadows
don't represent anything.
They're simply where
the light isn't.
Everyone
and everything
makes shadows,
but there's lots of light around
so it usually isn't serious.

Mountain

Born of bedrock, feet spread wide and strong,
warmth of magma flowing in your veins,
tall above the valley.

Granite loins where pine and fir stand proud,
wolf and wapiti, leaf and microbe, dance
their timeless minuet.

Below the chill winds curling round your breasts,
eagles soar with feather fingers spread
to grasp the playful air.

Whole among the wholeness, tiny giant,
atom in the cosmos, flash in time,
pause an endless instant.

Worn by blowing sand, your face is crumbling,
stooped by age, your snow-cloaked shoulders sinking
into an ancient sea.

In Memory of Seagulls

In memory of seagulls, we'll make a sign tonight
Dip the westward torch in fond salute
Strike fire from the clouds
Red burn the stratus
White heat the cumulous
Brush them from the forest tips
And echo them from the depths of the sea
Earth's evening mass and daily celebration
Sound above the voices of the mountains
A royal epitaph in memory of seagulls.

Scenario

A street   A leaden street without a name,
corner   A muted night
             With lonely footfalls carried on the wind

From darkness into darkness.
A solitary beacon blinks
Among deserted props and flats
From yesterday's matinee,
Blinks
and blinks

A bar   We few,
             We two
             (Where are the others?)

Sat while the ever-turning wheels of time
Spun silently,
Irresistibly,
And tired clocks (like tired minds)
Struggled to keep pace,
Sat behind a wall of glass
Sheltered from the wind.

Sat behind a wall of glass
Watching phantom faces pass
To and fro
Drifting through the dark outside
Caught on the night wind's febrile tide
Ebb and flow
Near yet distant dumbly hover
Cling like a rejected lover
Come and go

Sat
And talked
And laughed.Smoked
Countless cigarettes

And toyed with alcohol.
Doodled on the linen
Gestured with empty glasses,

Talked of books and plays, about
Beauty Truth and Sex and People.
Talked of Love and Gods, Infinity, Wine
And Society. Used terms we never could define:
Justified our existence
By our existence.
Safe from the night and the wind
and ourselves
We talked.

She turned her back
Soft-moulded back
To hear some chance remark,
Ran finely finished fingers through her hair
Hair that ruffles in the wind
Like spun walnut
Someone said "She's beautiful.
"Yes," I answered,
Fool! ------
 ------Fool I!,

That the satin of her cheek
Cool as a mountain stream to a dusty throat
The depth of her veiled eyes
Absinthe and Crystal lovingly blended
The curve of her thigh
Her breast
Her changeling smile
Dear Gods, don't let me love her
That these things that are her
can be described
As merely beautiful.
There is no word

A street The wheels of time spin on
Facing   Until another measureless measure of sand
the East Trickles through the fingers of the hand
      That stays the dawn.

A small We few
café   We two
      (Where are the others?)

Hid in a hole where the wind
Had blown us
Trying to bind ourselves together
With the last few wispy threads of gaiety
We'd brought with us:
Forced the conversation on
Knowing our time would soon be gone
While the strain showed under our eyes.
And outside

A doorway We two
      (Where are the others?)

Stood where a street lamp
Held the night at bay
Our faces white
In its eerie glow.
Halfway between the past and the future
Halfway between nowhere and infinity
We stood
Reluctant

A street And now
corner   Where are the others?,
      A ruthless wind carries lonely footsteps

Into the leaden night
And a beacon blinks.

Voices

Listen to the voices of the waves
call like children playing.
Listen to the voices of the waves
hear what they are saying.
Hide and seek
valley peak
some unique
softly speak
each of us the other.

Listen to the voices of the trees
Silent secrets sharing.
Listen to the voices of the trees
wisdom beyond caring.
Breathe and sigh
laugh and cry
live and die
tell you why
if you'll only listen.

Listen to the voices of the stars
faint beyond the sky flow.
Listen to the voices of the stars
sing outside your window.
Crystal chime
space and time
anthem climb
silent rhyme
harmony internal.

Chap 1

Isn't he beautiful, John
Mary murmured
Yes, I answered
holding our newborn child
soft in my shaking hands
He's alive, thank the Gods
in spite of unaccustomed
midwife me
assistant to the bride
Nor any doctor I could call
If there were another soul
alive on earth
she'd no more be a doctor
you can bet
than I am
which isn't saying much
It's a matter of observation
and deduction I suppose
with a knowledge of anatomy
thrown in
He's alive, I said
and that's beautiful
in itself.

And

One's not enough, I said
I know, she answered ---
I'd thought of that
but I didn't want to mention it
just yet
We'll be alright, I said
with a confidence I didn't feel
We'll have to bring them up
I said
to love each other a lot
And I guess we'll have to name
this one Adam
If you like, she said
though in her heart she'd have preferred
to crown him with the heavens
and call him Sun
She needed no touchstones
for security
She had the touchstones' wealth
personified, or so she thought
knowing I'd do my best to make it true
Maybe she'd just start
calling him Sun anyway
I'd catch on.

General Principles

General principles, a large but finite Universe,
so fast the change each day, each step is an adventure --
no signposts to the future but those we paint ourselves.

I serve Life, a student priest and bard.
The Ancients spoke to trees, to animals --
I speak to my computer, my car, my tools,
the food, the roof, for all these things have structure.

Life exists in Electron and Quark,
in Stone and Star and all of us between
and yet my mind the only channel that I know
through which to touch it.

Damn the false religions that have chained us!
They had their place in time, but now they drive us
to destruction and the ultimate insanity,
as do the myths of politics, culture and history,
outworn, outdated programs --
Garbage In - Garbage Out.

Statues

Men of bronze and men of stone
one of each from every generation, every war
stand in public parks, masquerade as art,

surrounded by their outworn tools of death,
commissioned by the men who didn't fight
to show the glory of their local war.

In stone is carved one man, the nation's hero
modelled as he'd like to be remembered,
carved the way we wish that he had been.

In bronze is cast the single face of many
in bronze the untold thousands who were slaughtered
Cast the way we wish that they had died.

Men of bronze and men of stone
one of each from every generation, every war
dressed up in the costumes of their station.

Men of stone are dressed in clothes for living
men of bronze are dressed in clothes for dying;
the fashions of the day.

Dog Food

When the men in the dog-food factory
told the computer
how many cans they'd sold that year

The computer told them back
that there weren't that many dogs
in the country

Which may be the first recorded incident
of social comment
by a machine.

Autumn

Summer's labour over,
warm autumn winds blow harvests of seed
from treetop to grass.

Daylight hours fading,
chill autumn winds blow harvests of leaves
from present to past.

Living colours dying,
cold winter winds blow harvests of snow
bring peace at last.

The 33d Floor

We are prisoners on the 33d Floor.
From our balconies we can look out
over the prison complex, row on row
of concrete towers and stucco walls.
We are let out twice a day to work
in the laundries or the machine shops,
to labour or to clerk for the wardens
and to buy with paper scrip
the food we cook for ourselves.

We are prisoners on the 33d Floor
behind rows of identical numbered doors,
the corridors named for the builder
or the nature destroyed in building.
We are let out twice a week to see
the ocean or the trees or attend
some propaganda cultural event.
Most times we watch the colored screen
that calms the mind and smothers thought.

We are prisoners on the 33d Floor
circumscribed by sameness and boredom.
To ease our frustration, we idle our time
with scrimshaw or with verse.
We are let out twice a life to fight
in wars and to attend the rites
that mark our passages into mating
and death -- our weddings and our funerals.

Free Fall

World without end, amen.
So let it be.
But all these things are relative,
everything connects
in reality or virtue
in sickness or in health
To the last syllable of reported time.

Speed of light, what then?
Perhaps we'll see,
but sight is indeterminate,
everything depends
on velocity or venue,
number or degree
To the last parable of recorded mind.

Dreams of flight pretend
that thought is free.
But all our words are literate.
Everything returns
in fantasy or echo,
in isomer or credo
to the last oracle of purported rhyme.

Early Memory

belly press hard to cold rock face
cling every digit to grainy surface
while waves crash my   tail
and winds drive me here, there
to drag me back into sea.
i will not go back.
i will climb in this cold stone
in spite of the wind and waves.
i will not go back
yet if I loosen grip of even
one   claw
fear wind will tear me loose
and weight of the earth will drag me down
and sea will have me.

this wall of gritty stone ends where?
i will know where,
yet in my fear i know
that my   strength is   short
i feel distant warnings from my body
hunger for life, for food
lest I weaken and lose my   grasp
and fall back into the cold and breathless
comfort of the waves.
I will not go back
and if I do it will be as dead meat
food for slithering things
that crawl the ocean floor.
I will not go back.
I will climb.
Up.

The ninth wave it has just receded.
For an instant there is a lull in the wind
and through the roiling gray above me
the sun and the moon lighten me
an infinitesimal amount.
I feel my chance
and holding fast with three claws,
let the other, the one beside my head,
spider up the rock, probing, groping
for a toehold, finger hold.

That's really all I remember.
But here I am
standing on my hind legs
with a glass in my hand,
and my eyes evolved so that
rather than swiveling independently
in a constant scan for danger,
they look forward,
and work together to give me a sense
of space and distance.

If you have the same memory
I'll assume we're related;
distant cousins perhaps,
and somehow drawn toward those tiny lights
in the chill winter sky.

Water Cycle

Sparkles in a highland spring
Flashes on the river
Ripples on an island beach
Thunder in the canyon,
Downland crossland growing still
Torrent raging onward
Fighting now we face the wind
Rolling down to leeward
Surge the seaquake of the tides
Wind-torn from the surface
Flung toward the ends of space
Pause in feather billows
Float in stony splendour there

Then dive and soar the long and windy road
That takes us home again as raindrops.

Ancestors

Around us
our ancestors flicker
in the play of light and shadow.
In the siffling of the wind
their voices, long dead,
whisper of times past
in half-forgotten words,
half remembered prayers.

Honour time, they say,
For this day will never come again ---
Once gone,
its memory will rush, spinning,
into the pages of unwritten history
of echoing thought.
This is a good day.
This is our day
to live.

Valley of the Shadow

As I walk through the valley of the shadow of life
Through pain and trouble and tears,
Where the road is hard and slow and I stumble as I go
Down a path that's seldom clear,
Where on every hand, some terror seems to stand,
And the dawn always seems so far away
I'll just keep going on and I'll pray the day will dawn
For there's really nothing else a man can do.

Among the rocks and trees, my mind forever sees
The shadows of the fears that follow me:
There are moments when I feel I can't tell what is real
And I'd trade my soul for light enough to see ---
And the brave songs that I sing seem to have a frightened ring
And my whistle in the dark is not too true ---
I'll go on another mile -- pray for Fortune's seldom smile,
For there is really nothing else a guy can do.

The wind is bitter cold and my coat is worn and old
And all ragged from the storms I've struggled through;
The sky is black with cloud and I wonder out aloud
If the wind will ever stop and let me be.
And my guts are so damn sore I can't manage one step more
And my body is all aching from the chill –
I'll go on another year and I'll pray in the sky will clear
For there's really nothing else a gal can do.

The people that I meet pass like shadows on a street
And not too many people pass this way;
I've heard their silent cries, I've looked deep into their eyes
And I've seen the loneliness reflected there.
For we're all alone, and find, imprisoned in our minds
We've no words for all the things we want to say --
I'll do the best I can – try and lend a helping hand
For there's really nothing else that we can do.

Though some corner of my mind knows there's nothing that I'll find
In whatever land this road will lead me to --
Though I know beyond this hill there's just another, steeper still,
And no signpost that will tell me how to go --
Though I know that in the end I may never meet a friend –
That among the shadows I must walk alone,
I'll go on a little way and I'll pray it soon is day
For there's really nothing else that I can do.

Perhaps some laughing gods are playing games, and laying odds
On whether or not I'll get through -- -- (break rhythm) NO! -- ---
--- --- --- --- --- --- --- whether or not WE' LL get through,
For I am just one face of the whole damn human race --
As a sorry sample, guess I'll have to do.
For I am only human, weak of heart and weak of hand
But in my weakness, there's a strength gods never know.
So don't stand in our way, or, Dear Gods, you'll find someday
There's really nothing humankind can't do.

Final Flight

The others had egged him on.
Astride his bike, penis erect, Jésus stormed
up the moonlit hill toward the town square.
To God and his Namesake, he said
If --- (pictured himself on the bike soaring over the iron post
and landing triumphant on the glistening cobbles), I will
 (candlelight picture of himself and the object of his passion,
barely yet a woman, kneeling at the altar rail).
Satisfied he said, God, you are a winner for accepting my promise.
The post grew in the pool of his headlight.
A wheel stumbled on the uneven cobbles,
and with a rising animal shriek, the bike soared
over the post and into the night. Beneath it
another animal flew, graceless, up-ended, toward the post.
It thought an instant prayer of acknowledgment to its God,
and a brief farewell to animal passion,
as the iron post inched incrementally nearer,
frozen in time.

What Have They Done to You

What have they done to you, my friend
that you have to stop me on the street?
What have they done to you, my friend
that you have to beg for something to eat?
Something to eat, something?

What have they done to your spirit, my friend
That your worn out shoes so timidly creep?
What have they done to your spirit, my friend
That you come to me for some place to sleep?
Someplace to sleep, someplace.

What have they done to your soul, my friend
that your sparkling eyes have lost their flame?
What have they done to your soul, my friend
that you come to me to discover your name
Find out your name, find out?

What have they done to your mind, my friend?
Are your thoughts too painful for you to think?
What have they done to your mind, my friend
that you come to me for something to drink?
For another drink, and another.

What have they done to your brain, my friend,
wine and whiskey puddiny pie?
What have they done to your brain, my friend,
that you come to me for some place to die,
someplace to die, someplace.

What have they done to me, my friend
that I have learned to hate you so well?
What have they done to me, my friend
that in your eyes I see my own hell?
My own ----

The Valley of Kings

Along the tree-lined avenue in royal triumphant ride,
My sword and scepter in my hand,
the cheering crowds on every side,
Last of my line, unwilling crown
from failing hands to me passed down,
The royal standard now is mine.
My father's word ruled in the land.
A royal dynasty he planned:
My father's word is my command.
My royal brothers' hearts are stilled,
their folded hands no longer toil;
Their bodies rest beneath the soil
Of the Valley of Kings.

Between my subjects' cheering lines, I nod my royal head
And smile my blessings to them all
where once before my brothers bled.
My brothers passed this way before me,
first in triumph, then in death
And now I search each face in turn,
And will my eyes to find the one
beneath whose coat there hides a gun
And the flash of light that hides the sun,
to end a dynasty of rule
by men like me, unwilling fool
Who was sworn to power while still a child,
My fate to meet a stranger's face:
to feel the chill of death's embrace
a puff of smoke, then take my place
In the Valley of Kings.

History will claim me and tell the way I died,
My name engraved in lasting stone,
a wave in time's relentless tide.
My guards surround me, weapons drawn,
but can they stop the gambit pawn --
The Hidden Masters' en passant,
With thirty silver phrases paid
to raise his hand against my life
With a bomb or a gun or a bloody knife,
While millions mourning weep and pray,
they'll carry me one final day
Down this tree-lined avenue
To the Valley of Kings.

Just the Same

You want the things he's offered you,
his money, car and name,
but you want my arms around you just the same.

His ring is on your finger,
and you play a loving game
but you want my arms around you just the same.

This double life you're living
can't to go on this way;
he's bound to discover
that you've lied to him (some day)

Though you hear the church bells ringing
it hasn't dimmed the flame,
and you want my arms around you just the same.

Game of Queens

In the hand that you've been dealt,
a pair of queens, but which one should you play,
the Queen of Diamonds or the Queen of Hearts?

On one queen bet a lifetime,
the other turn face-down and throw away,
the Queen of Diamonds or the Queen of Hearts?

Diamond Queen is calling you — golden is her voice,
Queen of Hearts just whispers low,
"Make love your choice. Make love your choice."

To choose between two fickle queens
two queens as different as are night and day,
the Queen of Diamonds?

Genesis

Flooded with sunlight, the silent lake mirrors cloudless, blue sky. The sand is radiant gold, a perfect summer's day. In the pool of shade under my tree I feel neither warmth nor coolness, and without thought or judgment, am the quintessential observer gazing at a scene suspended in time.

A boy walks past me carrying a fish. It is still alive, its gills swollen and pink, so perfect. And then I am in the utter blackness of endless space, no stars, no breath of solar wind. And I, the observer, disembodied, yet with my senses still intact, am sharing the consciousness of an entity just awakening, just born to awareness. And self-awareness — who, where, what, why am I? Then an imperative: Let there be light. But there was no light.

A moment, an age, an eon, passes, and the entity finds that she can create tiny particles out of space, out of nothing. To my perception they are the size and shape of a bean --- warm brown in color, and criss-crossed with two opposing spirals of tiny, iridescent dots; the particles don't glow, exactly, yet they are visible in front of me as if illuminated by a tiny hidden source of light. But they have mass, and the entity cannot not move them.

Another minute, age, eon, passes, and as the entity plays, she finds that she can make them spin, this way, that way. And if she spins one this way and the other one that way, they drift together, having some kind of mutual attraction. She makes several more, and of a sudden, there is a small, glowing sun — or atom — hovering in front of me. And it is good.

I'll make another one. And more particles appear and drift close together. But as they coalesce, the first tiny sun begins to fade and dim. Back to reanimate the first sun, but the second slowly begins to disperse.

Another moment, eon. I muse. Do I maintain my integrity or do I split and multiply myself, trusting that each of me will maintain the same vision. A moment passes and I choose. And then there are two suns, then four, and an explosion of suns and galaxies, spinning out in a stately dance to fill all space.

And I, the observer, am back on the beach, as the boy with the fish walks by and sunlight floods the lake.

Pilgrim

I am pilgrim, eternal pilgrim
time traveler in stranger lands
walking twisted roads and paths
beyond imagination, searching
among the rocks and shadows for
my own mythology, some truth
to comfort me amid my fears.

I am pilgrim, eternal pilgrim
carving paths through alien landscapes
feeling ways through moonless darkness,
screaming silence, always alone,
haunted by nameless, formless shadows
that claw from my imagination
and leave me helpless in my dreams.

I am pilgrim, eternal pilgrim
voyageur all lost upon the way
begging help from gods I know
only exist within myself,
star-eyed vision cursed by clouded sight
sensing past reason the gods of everywhere,
spirit giving form to universe.

I am pilgrim, eternal pilgrim
mindful errant bound upon the quest
willed to perseverance come what may,
holding course with purpose forged in will,
captain of life, life's servant, blazing trail,
leaving cairns and footprints in the dust
lest my brothers, sisters come this way.

Atman

There is this endless moment
someplace between death and rebirth,
a moment stretching on in endless agony,
or did the inner oracle speak truly
when she spoke of three --
three times the peaceful aching comfort
of the womb all warm within,
three times the burning anger to be born
-- -- to be united with one's self.

And if I am,
what else is there to die
except my body,
the temple tool
the Gods have fashioned for their work?

Ozymandias Reply to Shelley

As King of Kings, I need no mythic stranger
to make my epitaph a tidy rhyme.
My spirit soars beyond the desolation
that once proclaimed the triumph of my life:

Here fertile farms and thriving cities prospered
where proud and happy peasants cleared the forests
and channeled mighty rivers to their fields,
and neighbour nations cringed before my will.

Those centuries of wealth and peace and glory
have passed beyond the mountains of the sun,
but now my genes are scattered through the planet
waiting till my spirit lives again,

And once again I rise at history's bidding
to forge a greater empire on this plain.

Who?

Who stands against diffusion in the universe?
Who stands against the endless loss and leveling?
Who stands against the cosmic wind
that rips the molecules from lonely rocks and stars
and wears the silent mountains down?
Who captures stardust atoms, eons blown
beyond the reaches of the timeless dark?
Who stretches out to catch the heat
the suns have mindless wasted?
Who leaches from the earth and from the sea
the elements and compounds devious
sluiced from the streaming air by cloud-born rain?
Who takes the energy and matter
dissolved throughout the aether homogeneous
and calls them one
and gathers them
and feeds on them
and concentrates
and leave them there
still clinging to the rock in death,
my legacy of self to self
in change unchanging
when I am gone?

Main Street Anywhere

Main Street Anywhere. Who's to bother, who's to care?
Not the man of middle age whose years mount up despite his rage.
Horizon of his senile stage, treadmill squirrel in his cage
spends his money to forget his wife, his kids, his load of debt.
Double whiskeys fuel his jet to a tropic isle inside his head
where there's sunlight.

Main Street Anywhere. Who's to bother, who's to care?
Not the office-girl whose eyes, makeup-sparkle, studied, wise,
night by night and day by day seldom past her mirror stray.
Dreaming of a diamond ring, marriage to her stock car king,
takes a course on how to walk, lends her key and oils her lock
For good measure.

Main Street Anywhere. Who's to bother, who's to care?
Not the cop who pounds his beat secure he'll have enough to eat.
Hocks his brain and cocks his gun--- killing rats is sometimes fun.
Takes his pay to fill the jail and sit on the lid of the garbage pail.
But his feet hurt.

Main Street anywhere. Who's to bother, who's to care?
Not the man of means and power gazing at his garden flowers,
down the drive beyond the gate secure his home his fine estate,
chauffeur-driven twice a day (how can people live that way?)
Trophy wife, all giggles, thinks "let's ask the Windsors in the for drinks
After church."

Main Street Anywhere. Who's to bother, who's to care?
Not the Angel of the night beckoning by neon light,
peddling her holy wares, leads her john up creaking stairs.
Generations haven't changed her, instant love though she's a stranger
Hooked on fear or hung on horse, her cunt a court of last resource
for the loveless.

Main Street Anywhere, Who's to bother, who's to care?
Not the merchants in their stores leering from their pawnshop doors
selling bits of gaudy junk to hungry men who come in drunk.
Count their coin behind their hands, greed is all they understand,
bleed the marks — their profit gain from ten percent on human pain
plus interest.

Main Street Anywhere. Who's to bother, who's to care?
Not the politician's cat, furry sleek and purry fat,
who's never had to chase a mouse or spend a night outside the house.
Conversations he would know of law and order, status quo,
peasant pawns with minds to twist, statistics on a voters' list.
Lunch at the Toronto Club, roll over, have your tummy rubbed
and hunt from an armchair.

Main Street Anywhere. Who's to wonder, who's to care?
Not the academic world, cream-puff challenge bravely hurled:
angels pinhead dancing see steeped in obscure-ology.
objective, feel no guilt or shame; coolly allocate the blame,
published quibbles, tiny fame, make it right, give it a name
and dismiss it.

Main Street Anywhere. Who's to wonder, who's to care?
Not the Revolutionary, power-ploy incendiary --
wells of human suffering mine to swell the propaganda line,
upside down the world ideal, ignorant believe it's real.
Yours is not to reason why, yours is to destroy and die.
Building up isn't your department.

Main Street Anywhere. Who's to bother, who's to care?
Village blasted burnt and black, kidnapped children don't come back.
Father, old and impotent waves a stick at where they went,
asks the wordless question why fire thunders from the sky.
Are the gods angry?

Main Street Anywhere. Who's to wonder, who's to care?
Paper boats in gutters sunk: flotsam, jetsam, human junk
litter sidewalks, clutter bars, crumbling buildings, rusting cars,
claw through life without a guide not knowing why they're born or die
never know the rules of the game, die reluctant just the same.
They've no place else to go.

Main Street anywhere. Who's to bother, who's to care?
The little time we have we clutch horizons close enough to touch.
Confused, deluded empty souls can only seek our lonely goals
and lie in fetal posture curled. Don't bother me about the world
I've troubles of my own.

Trinity in Space
(after Gwendolyn MacEwan)

Beyond the distant stars and constellations
Where speed-of-light and stasis are the same,
You drift alone in silent space, a trinity –
Trembling, tattered child embraced by solitude,
Adult imprisoned in a lonely egg,
Buddha, one-hand raised in soft applause.

This is not the holy place you searched for:
beyond the reach of wavelength, angle, vector;
you sought to touch the minds of the Divine,
clarity's insight, welcome warmth of home.

But now you are three, one with fingers bloody
from tearing culture's tough resilient fabric,
while child and Buddha, impotent and nerveless,
Watch and dream of unity.

One Two Three Infinity

Object and reflection mirror each other,
height reflected on a floor of mirror sea,
depth reflected on a ceiling mirror sky,
the sky below
the sea above
caught in stasis equilibrium
where gravity impels you to the deep
and buoyancy will call you to the sky.
But conquer one
and become two,
the high and the deep
and when the ripples of your passing have receded
the world that's still expanding
as it shrinks upon itself,
you pass beyond the centre
to the surface
to become three
and finally
infinity.

Stranger

Tell me, Mr. Stranger, in the mirror on the wall,
Your face is quite familiar but your name I can't remember.
Was it Truro in the springtime
Or Vancouver in the flight from Montreal?
Where('re) you going? Where you been?
Notify your next-door neighbour
Long time gone.

Tell me, Mr. Stranger in the mirror by the sink,
Your teeth are getting longer but your eyes don't seem to waver.
Was it high-school in September
Or the bars we used to haunt till the last call?
What'cha doin'? What'cha done?
Who's your parents' favourite baby?
Long time gone.

Tell me, Mr. Stranger in the mirror by the door,
Your hair is getting greyer and it's thinner than becomes you.
Was it workin' in the city
Or just soakin' up the sunshine on the shore?
What'cha givin'? What'cha got?
What'cha missin'? Thanks for nothin',
Long time gone.

Coffee House Angel

Don't go walking through Steeltown
with a coffee-house angel:
She'll lead you down by the railroad yards
and leave you all alone.

There's something unreal
about a coffee-house angel:
she'll keep you hot while you've got a lot
to give, but when the money's gone,

Coffee house angels – they're all the same:
when they don't need you they'll leave you
with nothing – not even your name.

There's something unreal
about a coffee-house angel.
She'll keep you high until she's bled you dry
But after you come down
It's a different town.

Teacher

Calmly in front of her class,
controlling by subtle changes
in voice --- softer, louder,
faster, slower, conscious of time,
of herself, her beauty.

Demonstrates correctness,
draws attention to pretty, high-arched feet
rounding buttocks in fleecy panties,
strong legs, graceful lordosis,
seeks love among her students.

Hair severe goes home
through the trellised vulval gate
of her fortress fence,
up birth-canal walkway
to red, red womb front door.

In one fallopian tube
processes private clients
healing, advising
with calm authority
sends them, reborn, into the street
and their own lives.

In the morning,
serving Yahweh, Shiva,
she descends, herself reborn
from her own red, red womb.

Poets' Night

Like droplets of cream drifting in a sea of coffee
One by one they rise and speak their piece,
Artful careless dun-hued earthen costume,
Humble, self-effacing, each unique.
No odysseys, no swords in stone, no fantasy,
No star-crossed lovers, princesses or queens:
Just Harlequin in autumn-tinted motley
And Columbine in mustard-coloured dreams
Where kitchens merge with lands of ancient mythos,
Where pain and passion torment our humanity,
Where gardens bloom with pumpkins, beans and roses
And commonplace is etched in acid clarity.
But what of those who witness this commission?
They also serve who only sit and listen.

Blue lights

Blue light, an endless patterns repeating
shine in glowing cathedral darkness
transparent to stars
a space in space.

Light waves of white caps of stars
rush through the mouth of the cave
a feather-soft surf
evaporates lightly
flows back so quietly
leaving inviolate
this place in place.

Light shafts rebound, echo like sound
reflections from matter substance insubstantial
formed into craglets
inter-grace facelets
formed by the flashing
of light upon nothing
darkness beyond
in darkness rebounding
face interface.

Cosmic Explorer

(dedicated to Dr. Francine Grace)

Out upon the cosmic wind, they sent me as a child,
dressed in steel with lightning boots,
a thousand light-years at a stride,
and I traveled and I traveled far beyond a thousand suns --
long forgotten in the distance, the place where morning "rises."
And I've walked a thousand planets
and I've searched a thousand moons;
I've seen leaf veins carved in fossil rock
where not a leaf or lichen grew.
Gone the gentle grass that answers
when the morning breezes whisper.
And on a few, I've seen a trace of straight lines in the sand -
crumbling stone, corroding steel,
erased by time's relentless hammer,
and on some, the sun burned low.

Now I'm back to tell my children (grandchildren many times removed)
the answers to the questions their parents trusted me to fathom.
And I'm old now, and I'm old now, and my hair is thin and gray,
and the children I grew up with generations passed in silence.
And I've climbed a thousand mountains
and I've walked a thousand plains.
I've seen leaf veins carved in fossil rock
where not a leaf or lichen grew:
gone the gentle grass that answers
when the morning breezes whisper.
And on a few I've seen a trace of straight lines in the dust --
crumbling stone, corroding steel, returned to chaos as they must,
and the lamp of life burns low.

I'll find a place that's warm and sheltered, by the sea,
far beyond the poison cancer of the cities' madness.
And I'll wait there, and I'll wait there till the Gods have gone away
from this image of their failure. And when I shit I'll pray
And I'll wed a thousand oceans and I'll seed a thousand waves -
I'll dream leaf veins carved in fossil rock
where not a leaf or lichen grows.
I'll dream the gentle grass that answers
when the morning breezes whisper,
and on this earth I'll leave a trace of straight lines in the soil --
crumbling bone, corroding flesh
to ease my childrens' timeless hunger,
and I'll start the dance anew.

Winterland

Winterland, where falling stars meet morning's glow,
I walk a land of silent snow,
crystal tears of frozen dew.
Lonely, you're here and rainbows fill my eyes;
I couldn't stay and you know why,
in Winterland the flowers cry.

Winterland, and now I'm midwife to the Sun,
the morning's labor has begun
born from out the womb of night.
Wonder where I'm going, where I've been
and what the changeling date may bring.
Will Winterland be ever spring?

Winterland, and now the snow has turned to rain;
sun hangs veiled in mists of pain
the things we said when last we kissed.
Weeping, morning sky sheds bitter tears,
the ones I've disciplined for years.
In Winterland, nobody hears.

The Serpent

AyeeAyeeAyeeAyeeAyeeAyeeAyee am the SSSSerpent (ooahaha),
SSSSSSSSSSSSSSSSsssssssssssssssssSent by the Devil (mwahahah)
SSSsilently at midnight, joyfully in ssssssuuuunlight,
SSSSSSSSSSSSSSSSsssssssssssssssssStriking at the maAaAaAaAinds
Of your wives and your children.

AyeeAyeeAyeeAyeeAyeeAyeeAyee am the SSSSerpent (Hya Hya Hya)
SSSSSSSSSSSSSSSSsssssssssssssssssssSorcerer and pilgrim (HooHooHaha)
SSSSSSSSSSHSHSHSSHSHHSHSHSHining up the Apple
Of wisdom and knowledge of good and EEEEEvil
And I shall make you freeEE EE EE EE EE and I shall make you gods.
YAHAHAHAH yyuha heee heeee etc.

AyeeAyeeAyeeAyeeAyeeAyeeAyee am the SSSserpent
Listen to me Adam,
AyeeAyeeAyeeAyeeAyeeAyeeAyee am the SSSserpent
Listen to me, Madame,
AyeeAyeeAyeeAyeeAyeeAyeeAyee am the SSSerpent,
Just call me VIPER –ER –ER –ER –er –er—er –er
I'm a V.I.P. !!!
YA HA HA HA HA HA , HOOHAH HOOHAH YAHEE etc. ad.lib.

The Moment

When you live on a boat, Filly Girl, there is a moment
that you live a thousand times, each one unique
yet all the same. There is a moment when
you leave each remembered port where they all
blur into one ---- into one movement of your hand
and the feelings that tear you.

There is a moment when you walk down the jetty
on a calm morning and climb aboard
and blow the bilges and fire the engines
and wait until they idle smoothly, and cast off the lines ---
There is a moment when you stand at the helm,
engines softly chuckling, and the weather is fair
and the fresh, offshore breeze has drifted you
alee the dock.

There is a moment when you savour the warmth you are leaving,
and the comfort and safety of the harbour.
There is a moment of excitement as you face the open water
and open sky where the wind caresses your cheek
and sunlight sparkles the wavelets with promise
of new ports, new friends and new life,
And the fear of the storm and the waves, and the chilling bite
of icy rain and the loneliness of the sea.

There is a moment when you feel all these things
the joy and the regret of love forever lost,
of trust and trust broken, of the brighter hope
for something new, and the disappointment
of more of the same.

There is a moment when you will your hand
to grasp the gearshifts and push them gently forward
until they engage   and you feel the slight bump
as the propellers take hold,
and the change   in the rhythm   of the engines
and the faint gurgle of your wake. And . . .

There is a moment when you know you dare not look back,
to a flimsy wharf where smiles may mean nothing
where questions are many but answers few.
For only in a desert wilderness of wind and waves
can you seek what is really in your heart   and know
that if you return, it will be for right reasons
with no preconceptions, hopes or expectations.

There is a moment
when you know that the search for perfection is futile.
And yet, in matters metaphysical,
which have no mass or weight, but only velocity,
why not? In seven days you will be leagues
away, and you will not look back without
a meditation of solitude because you know
your resolve might weaken as you face the vast
terror of the heavens and the timeless
distances between the stars.

There is a moment when you know that what is done
is done, and that the observer absorbs the radiation
where her shadow falls and for an instant
obscures the stars, so that something small
forever changes.

Try a Little Persecution

If you want to move some people to a far-off land,
Try a little persecution.
If you want to make some people do the things you've planned
Try a little persecution.
If you want to turn some peasants into pioneers,
To labour in a wilderness of trouble, toil and tears,
Then kill a few and burn a few and work upon their fears
As you try a little persecution.

If you want to build a nation in some barren soil
Try a little (some religious) persecution.
If you want to waste a million lives in thankless toil,
Try a little persecution.
If you want to move some people off their lazy butts
To live out in a desert waste in tents or freezing huts,
Then martyr some and torture some and give a few the gears
As you try a little persecution.

If you want to build an empire that will last a thousand years,
Try a little persecution.
Or colonize a galaxy while you bring up the rear,
Try a little persecution.
If you want to move some people off their sofas and their chairs
To live out on some planet where there isn't even air --
America or Israel, the Arctic or the Moon --
Try a little persecution.

To a Sea Monster

aye aye

no no

trills

maaaaOooooth

CHOKED!

by the seaweed of your Sargasso slime,

you drift abloat,

surrounded by listing

hulk hulk

 hulk   hulk

    hulk

hulk hulk

  hulk

of clippers traders men-o'war and pirates
whose foolish captains
(now grinning gritting gristling skeletons)
once threw you a line.

Now you savour the memories of your sly saliva OratOr's tongue
lasciviously licking, lovingly lapping their lovely necks
before your reptile jaws CRUSHED their hornpipes
and SUCKED their sweet, sweet spirit

(May Goddess in Her love and mercy bless
all hearts of oak who sail the ocean's wilderness)

(The Girl on the) 16th Floor

The view from the 16th floor is beautiful and different.
Signs and symbols shroud the city down below
where the silent streets in chessboard order,
black and white their distant borders,
hide the colours she used to know
a long time lifetime yesterday ago.

And she sits in her window on the 16th floor,
her image in the glass reflected clear.
Painted there on the city it's really her outside —
it's only her reflection here in the chair.
Mirror-smashed her jigsaw face,
pieces that won't fit in place,
a madonna trapped insider her stained-glass window,
her castle dreams all crumbling sand,
the echoes of the years she'd planned
left hanging like an uncompleted sentence.

And she sits in her window on the 16th floor
and finger-counts the cost of fairy wishes.
In the waiting room outside tomorrow's life, an unlocked door,
she sits and leafs anew through her back issues —
lingers here and looks behind
to chart the labyrinths of her mind
and wander through the ruins of her childhood
when she was at an awkward age
and young and going through a stage
that people said she someday would grow out of.

And she sits in her window on the 16th floor
and shares the diamond song of her own weeping,
dressed up in her memories of the world she's left behind
where poverty's the only vow worth keeping,
looking backwards all the way,
her arms stretched out to yesterday
and only blind gods know where she is going,
so pardon her if she should cling
to every thought and anything
that keeps it real for just another morning.

The view from the 16th floor is beautiful and different,
but that was a long time, lifetime, yesterday ago.

ASTRA

Astra
Astra, Astarte
star-scattered beauty,
Nuit sky arching over me
beckons in whispering thunder
release the earth and rise to join me
with arms outstretched, flooded with love
and devotion I rush slowly to her stardust arms.
Humbled as we float in space, I embrace her in fivefold kiss.
no dry ritual this but all the love my hands my lips my tongue can
speak. Soft hollows of her knees, smooth, firm thighs, gently kiss, lick,
cup her breasts, sculpt comet-speckled areolas, nipples gently
gripped between my teeth our mouths are limpet locked.
Breath flows back and forth between us, through
awe-struck O's to lovingly suckle life from one
another then give it back and more demanding
lips grip me fiercely within the inverse
cosmic globe, to draw me to
her core while her breasts
softly, succulently, melt
through my ribs to enfold my heart.
Universe begins to swell and quake, Oh, how can I tell you, echo
from planet to planet throughout the timeless reaches of space
giant suns flicker and dim
and stumble weakly
in their orbits.

In celestial peace ivy twine, dream dancing,
spoon and merge she and I together watch
my ancient persona shell, socialized man,
fall away, an empty, crumpled suit of clothes,
drifting forever between cradling galaxy arms.

New understanding, love, gaze fondly back
at Earth and her creatures. For the moment
we are content, searching idly for the living spark
who, spreading fresh wings, will be our next lover.

Mindquake

hear the rush of electrons through the cosmos on
an ordinary day they're talking on the radio
you're picking something up from the table when
suddenly reality trembles time shakes the
universe shudders and dissolves the buildings
blur and double pastel peach and gray windows
forgotten in silent thunder.

and then it's over nothing changed nothing
the same all new all over space warp reality
shift time travel.

let's see, they were saying there's no scientific
way to define race yeah we know that but we all
use the concept and know what we mean but they
weren't talking about that and then this guy
making a point about something else entirely
says in passing as a given
that the two world wars were just civil wars
within the white race
and the rest of the program was irrelevant
so is everything else.

Leo's Quest

When Leo was a little boy they kept him in a place
where he couldn't see the mountains and he couldn't see the sea.
The people all around him were so caught up in their race
that they couldn't see the mountains, and they couldn't see the sea.
They packaged him in underwear and sent him off to school;
they filled his head with oatmeal and a thousand iron rules;
and they spoke to him in silence, and they made him feel a fool
when he asked about the mountains and wondered 'bout the sea.

When Leo was an older boy they told him not to play
any games about the mountains -- any songs about the sea.
The mountains were forbidden and the sea too far away,
so forget about the mountains and pretend there is no sea.
They filled his ears with sealing wax and said the world was flat;
they cut his hair like Samson's and they made him wear a hat,
and they brought him up their model of where the world was at:
a world without the mountains and a world without the sea.

When Leo was a teen-age boy, they took away his heart
so he'd never miss the mountains and he'd never need the sea.
They told him it was wrong for anyone to stand apart
and gaze upon the mountains, and contemplate the sea.
They took away his personhood as if it were a vest,
they bound him with a mortgage and chained him to a desk
and they blinded him with neon signs and told them it was best
that he never see the mountains and never know the sea.

When Leo was a young man he met a mad guru
who whispered of the mountains and chanted of the sea.
At first he could not hear him, then he let his mind flow through,
and he learned about the mountains and heard about the sea.
He saw the iron chains that bound him in the lonely crowd;
he opened up his collar, and he learned to sing out loud;
and he flew to the horizon, there to stand up proud
and look upon the mountains, and gaze upon the sea.

So Leo did his Sundance and I know that you can, too,
if you really want the mountains and really need the sea.
You'll find the sea will open and the mountains come to you
if you're hungry for the mountains and thirsty for the sea.
The way is not an easy one -- you blaze trails as you go,
as mighty rivers carve themselves the courses that they flow.
The first step is the hardest, but someday you may know
what it's like to scale the mountains and sail upon the sea.

To an Ancient Goddess

Granite eyes bruised by wind-blown sand
and washed by centuries of stormy tears,
You gaze out on a flickering twilight landscape
where swirling moons streak by in heartbeat space
and stars glow dimly in the constant dusk,
as season cycles melt from spring to winter
in the turning of a hand. It is a miracle
that generations of the tiny creatures,
no taller than Your ankle, even conceived You,
never mind constructing You from quarried
stone, their only tools their naked hands.

By labour imbued with their collective Divinity,
champion of all their common dreams,
embodying the sum of all their will,
You changed the pattern of the vagrant winds
and moved the clouds that drift before the sun
to nourish fields of grain with gentle showers
and make the bitter winters less severe.
And so You watched their cities rise and crumble
and mourned the trees retreating to the mountains.
Now few children come to bring You flowers:
your strength to sway the winds is almost gone.

Yet now new people come from distant places
to marvel at Your makers' victory
of bare hands over stone, to build a lasting
Image of their love and their devotion.
Drawing inspiration from Your grandeur
and making flashing images for memory,
they take Your icons home with their returning
and spread Your fame for all the world to know.
Thus millions now will grant You newfound power
to alter once again the winds' direction
and make the fields and forest bloom anew.

Girl

How the days go drifting by; sun hangs heavy in the sky,
autumn colours make my eyes go crazy.
Friends and lovers I once knew fade away like the morning dew
and everything except for you seems hazy.
Girl, where are you leading me? What have you done to me?
Now that you're one with me, love has come to me.
This is not the life I'd planned, but here we wander hand-in-hand,
drifting through a lovely land of daisies.

Safe inside an iron ring, I'd never heard a robin sing
nor felt the morning's glories climb around me,
but since you came into my life to be my lover, friend and wife
you've opened up the iron ring that bound me.
Girl, why did you wait so long to make my life a song?
This time I can't be wrong; I feel your love so strong,
and every time I think of you I wonder what I'd ever do
if you'd never come along and found me.

Oaths are brittle nowadays, and no one but a fool would say
that nothing can a love decay or sever,
but loving you the way I do and knowing that you love me too
I'm almost brave enough to try for never.
Girl, where am I leading you? If there's a love that's true
it's mine for you -- I know you need me too.
Through hidden years that lie ahead, one word rings inside my head:
as best we know the word, we've said forever.

That's How you Feel Today

You whispered a name in the shadow of a moment
then you wondered where the glow went
when the first cold flakes of snow went
by the Milky Way. That's how you feel today.
Warm tender breasts, the bursting of buds of springtime,
but the bitter leaves of autumn have been blowing all around you
in the wind today.
That's how you feel today.

A thousand mornings in your sight are but a moment gone
-- that's how you feel.
A thousand aching memories will haunt you
in the early morning dew.
Timeless your smile -- for you can be no sorrow
for the wine of gods you've borrowed -
but how many proud Tuesday mornings
have you turned away, just why you couldn't say.
That's how you feel today.

You search for your name in this shadow-land you've found,
your voice the strangest sound --
you're crazy world has stopped inside you
heaven seems to sway -- That's how you feel today
Visions of the Gods, infinity's horizon,
now you've turned your golden eyes on countless galaxies inside one
living piece of clay.
That's how you feel today.

Winging through the cosmos by the pale stars' lonely tracks
to seek what's real
where tiny suns are playthings and the mountains melt like wax,
that's how you feel.
But how many nights have your tears stained strangers' shoulders
while your world keeps getting older and your heart of ash burns gray
So, act their little play if you must,
but you'll pick the role you play, I trust,
'cause that's how you feel today.

For Alice

When I consider all the days we've spent
together and the countless ways you've lent
your warmth and strength to thirty-something years --
for almost half my lifetime and as much
or more than that of yours,
I know that I will die while you're still young
with many years of life to still enjoy
with mind and body, sight and senses bright.
Remember me with kindness and when then

my ashes are returned to Goddess Earth
who only loaned them to me for a day,
my memory may linger softly in your ken
forgotten in the depths of space and then
a flash of time as I am gone away.

So then, as now, I trust that you'll be free
to love as chance and circumstance decree.

For Every Road

For every road you travel there's another road you'll never take.
For every place you ramble there's another place that you can't stay.
You'll see the seasons come and go,
you'll watch the years just melt away like snow
and then you'll know.

For every hill you climb on there's another hill you'll never see.
For every meal you dine on there's a meal that's ceased to be.
I've seen the sky and touched the land,
I've heard the ocean breakers thunder on the sand
and I think I understand --

For every one you love there's another love you'll never know.
For every flower you pluck there's a place no flowers grow.
We use the precious days that we've been lent
We make our choices and when we've counted up
how much we've spent,
may we be content.

([instrumental] bridge)

For every world you plunder there's another world you'll never make.
For every day you slumber there's a day you won't awake.
You'll see the seasons come and go.
You'll watch the years just melt away like snow
and then you'll know.

Religious Limericks

Moses, oh Moses, my friend,
when will this slavery end?
You've struck and you've stopped
and you've ruined the crops
but you'll have to bear arms in the end.

The digger next door was undressing,
for the purpose of David impressing
so ethics be damned
he offed her old man
and awaited the Adonai's blessing.

Mary, O Mary, old girl,
why don't we give it a whirl
and if there's a baby
we'll tell them that maybe
he's son to all men in the world.

Jesus, O Jesus, I've heard
that you've been described as The Word.
A word is a thimble
of knowledge - a symbol
by which an idea's transferred.

Pontius Pilate, you fool,
chosen as history's tool,
famous through time
your hand-washing crime,
you're the archetype of small men who rule.

Shaitan's Gospel Song

Is your heart obsessed with fear? Crushed by lonely hunger?
Listen to the angel chorus sing their favorite number:
Jesus, Jesus, safe in the arms of Jesus,
father, mother, lover, child,
all in one are reconciled
safe in the gentle, loving arms of Jesus.

Sing the angel chorus high, glory hallelujah,
one man lives while thousands die -- justify it to you.
Jesus, Jesus, safe in the arms of Jesus,
our long years with yours we buy --
yours the souls that sooner fly
safe to the gentle loving arms of Jesus.

Does the future wear you down? Is your lot to worry?
Rest your burden on the ground, there's no need to hurry.
Jesus, Jesus, safe in the arms of Jesus,
hocus-pocus dominocus,
listen to the words that choke us
safe in the gentle loving arms of Jesus.

View the few who have it all, billions haven't any
come and hear the Savior's call -- we'll accept your widow's mite.
Jesus, Jesus, safe in the arms of Jesus,
Blessed be thy discontent --
won't you help us pay our mortgage?
safe in the gentle loving arms of Jesus.

Structure in the curse of time, hierarchies ascending
help us up, we'll pull you down, (to) hellfire never ending.
Jesus, Jesus, safe in the arms of Jesus,
echoes of the patriarchs,
morals drawn from Noah's Ark
safe in the gentle loving arms of Jesus.

Sales promotion pays its way, won't you kindly offer
gold and frankincense and myrrh to help us fill our pockets.
Jesus, Jesus, safe in the arms of Jesus,
swiftly swings the autumn moon,
Be prepared to meet him soon
Safe in the gentle loving arms of Jesus.

In the castles of the land, pirate, noble, squire
take and take till poor men break -- hire us as they're liars.
Jesus, Jesus, safe in the arms of Jesus,
on the altar of his love,
grease our palms, don't soil our gloves
safe in the gentle loving arms of Jesus.

Fashions Change

Fashions change, created for a season.
There is no rhyme or rhythm:
Meteors will blow away as dust.
This year skirts are longer or the other way around.
Smack and crack are in, or is it smoke and alcohol?
My compass can't recall what year it is —
rollerblades or Rolling Stones
And Shakespeare's not as young as he used to be
Or is it you? Or is it me?
But if you ask, I'll tell you how it's going to be next year —
What you'll do and who you'll love and
what you'll wash and wear.
But change and progress aren't the same
As Fashions Change.

Fashions Change, created for a season:
There is no rhyme or reason,
Iceberg tips in sunlight melt to mist.
This year hair is longer or the other way around.
This year girls love boys, or is it Love Each Other Week?
My Calendar won't say what place this is:
Renaissance or Babylon
and Jesus isn't in the inn today.
Or is it you, or is it me?
But if you ask, I'll tell you what you're going to do next year:
How you'll live and how you'll love and
how you'll wear your hair.
But Change and Progress aren't the same
As Fashions Change.

Fashions Change, created for a reason:
There is no time or season;
autumn leaves in splendor burn to ash.
This year legs are longer or the other way around.
Breeding is the answer. No, environment's the key.
My watch just can't reveal what day this is —
Ecology, Astrology,
And Bucky Fuller came a different way
Or was it you? Or was it me?
But if you ask I'll tell you the economy next year:
How you'll survive and who you'll screw and
what's your biggest fear.
But change and progress aren't the same
As Fashions Change.

In a concert scored for radio, magazines and video
recordings, news, the media are weaving an illusion
that things are really changing
by calling everything a different name,
though everything is really just the same
in a circus chimed on neurotape, tetraphonic audioscape
Internet in digital stroboscopic alpha wave
multiscreen in binary modulated mantram hum,
neon mythic metronome,
But change and progress aren't the same
As Fashions Change.

Dream World

Dream World inviting, wild moon is burning
starlight is tinkling over the dewdrops once more,
Warm waves of light wash ashore
see what your dreams have in store.
Soft golden fountains burst into mountains,
drift into fine silver words that dissolve in the night,
footsteps of legions of light, pathways of sparkling delight.
Warm April laughter that flows on the rooftops
of thresholds of thousand years old,
arches of Crystal dissolve in a forest
of candle-flames dripping with gold.
Pinwheel crescendos blossoming into
circles in circles enshrined on an altar of time,
flashes of childhood design, echoes distilled into wine.

Dream World oasis shimmering faces,
heartbeats suspended still frozen in time to be born,
trumpets that savage the morn,
bronze stands the huntsman forlorn.
Stone masks of ages, fairytale pages
created a flickering sand-castle stories of kings,
silence on carnival wings, song breath of tenderness clings.
Cruel liquid jewels a tunnel of gladness
where elf-lamps in perfumed desire,
fragments of sunlight weave Persian grass carpets
in gardens all flowers of fire.
Soon you'll be waking, Dawn will be breaking,
I will be taking my leave of you tip-toe away
into the crucible day, but for one moment to stay.

Dream World, time's ocean, cosmos in motion,
swept through the sea-caves of consciousness tide
back from a fairyland ride,
back to the world of outside.

Wandering

I'm walking down the road again, drifting from town to town,
I'm walking down the road again, trying to find direction
I get weary wandering the highways
I get weary wondering if I'll ever find a place to call my home
In an old stone house or a geodesic dome.
I'm walking down the road again,
Just wandering, wondering, wandering.

I'm sailing down a stream again, drifting from place to place.
I'm sailing down the stream again, trying to see my reflection.
I get weary wandering the waterways.
I get weary wondering if my boat, will ever touch the shore
And I wish I had a rudder or an oar.
I'm sailing down the stream again,
Just wandering, wondering, wandering

I'm soaring on the wind again, drifting from cloud to cloud
I'm soaring on the wind again, trying to find perfection.
I get weary wandering the skyways.
I get weary wondering
if I'll ever find another bird that sings --
One that I can fly with wing to wing
I'm soaring on the wind again,
Just wandering, wondering, wandering.

Childhood's End

Softly the winds of the morning open our embrace
at Childhood's End.
Blue-gold, a new day is dawning: dew-mist kisses your face
at Childhood's End.
The bridge of tears between us is far too long to cross
and yet my heart is burning like the sun.
Firmly the Book of Changes turns another page
at Childhood's End.

Silent you stand before me, hands outstretched to mine
at Childhood's end.
Smiling, your eyes explore me with tears of bitter wine
at Childhood's end.
The love our hearts are crying out for isn't ours to give
and yet your heart is glowing like the moon.
Surely this bitter fruit will wither on the vine
at Childhood's End.

Fiercely by winds of fortune scattered 'cross the sky
At Childhood's End.
High above the timeless ocean, free gulls you and I,
at Childhood's End.
Far beyond the cloudrace and the fevered forest shore
we'll learn to bend the four winds to our will,
and someday we'll find our heart-homes
on some sun-drenched hill
at Childhood's End.

Benediction

If humankind can't walk upon the sea
let them walk upon the land.
If humankind can't choose a way that's free
let them choose the place to make their stand.
Must they go back the way they came
on hands and knees back to the trees?
If humankind can't choose the way they'll live
let them choose the way they'll die.

A Program Note

THE POEMS AND LYRICS in this book were inspired by Shakespeare, Burns, both Brownings, Milton, Millay, Poe and Noyes, and contemporaries like Ian, Gordy, Stan, Pete, Judy, Tom and Joni, and were composed for performance as sung- or spoken word, either for an audience or in the privacy of a bedroom or a forest clearing. I have been initiated and spontaneously declared a poet and a bard, but I think of myself as a hedge bard and folk performer.

Many of these verses worked well as songs, but after I'd lived with them for a while I found that speaking them freed them (and me) from the enforced discipline of rhythm, melody and the guitar. When I perform nowadays, I do both. I have lead sheets for many of them, and a few CDs (Copyright registrations go back to 1967).

About the Author

TED MacGILLIVRAY, born in Toronto Ontario, attended Waycroft School, Upper Canada College and Parkdale C.I. with prizes in Science and Dramatic Verse. He studied theatre with Robert Gill at Hart House Theatre (University of Toronto), voice with Charles Jordan, guitar with Elli Kastner and Tony Braden and has attended Buckminster Fuller's World Game Workshop in Philadelphia. He appeared in plays at Hart House, with the Toronto Alumnae, and in musicals at the Royal Alexandra. He has toured Canada performing his own and others' work, and has appeared in two of Canada's major folk festivals, Winnipeg and an early Mariposa, where he was master of ceremonies and artistic director. He was a director of a Toronto YMCA folk-music educational program and was MC and narrator of 'Canada's Story in Song' at the Toronto Exhibition Bandstand.

He has worked in private radio as a writer and announcer, in advertising agencies (radio/TV producer/production supervisor) and in television as news editor and cameraman, as well as writing and directing several documentary films for private industry and for broadcast by the CBC. He was a cultural interpreter at the Pioneer Village, the media coordinator for Alberta Parks' Kananaskis Country, was on the staff of the Canadian Broadcaster and Telescreen, has written a weekly column for the *Canmore Miner*, and was editor of *Sing and String* (a folk-music publication) and the *Automotive Digest*. He is an ordained Wiccan priest.